THE HEART OF THE MATTER

NAVIGATING CHILDREN'S MENTAL HEALTH WITH CLARITY AND COMPASSION

Dr. Faisal Ahmed, MD

Board-Certified Child and Adolescent Psychiatrist

California

PREFACE

There is a question I find myself returning to again and again, after decades of sitting across from children and their families in my office in California: How can we love someone so deeply and still understand them so little?

It is not a criticism. It is simply the truth of parenthood — and one of the most human experiences there is. We live in an age overflowing with information. We can search any symptom, stream any parenting philosophy, and find an expert opinion within seconds. And yet, so many parents still feel lost. Overwhelmed. Unsure whether what they are seeing in their child is typical development or something that deserves a closer look.

That gap — between the information that exists and the understanding parents actually carry into their daily lives — is what inspired this book.

I am Dr. Faisal Ahmed, a board-certified child and adolescent psychiatrist practicing in California. Over the course of my career, I have worked with children at every stage of development, from wide-eyed toddlers taking their first uncertain steps toward independence, to teenagers navigating identity crises and emotional storms that shake the whole family. I have sat with parents who were terrified, exhausted, grief-stricken, and deeply confused. And I have watched, time and again, as understanding — real, practical, compassionate understanding — changed everything. That is what I set out to offer here.

The first half of this book is devoted to the foundation: how children grow. Not just physically, but emotionally, cognitively, and socially. I have always believed that you cannot truly recognize what is wrong until you understand what is right. Before we can speak meaningfully about anxiety, ADHD, trauma, or mood disorders, we need a clear picture of what healthy development looks like at each stage — what is normal for a 2-year-old, a 7-year-old, a 14-year-old — and why. That context changes everything about how we respond to our children.

The second half turns to the harder conversations: mental illness in children and adolescents. These are subjects that carry far too much stigma and far too little plain-spoken guidance. Conditions like ADHD, autism, depression, anxiety, bipolar disorder, and the aftermath of childhood trauma are not rare. They are sitting in classrooms, at dinner tables, and in the quiet bedrooms of millions of families right now. They deserve to be spoken about clearly, accurately, and without shame.

Throughout these pages, I have tried to write the way I speak with families in my office — directly, honestly, and with genuine warmth. There is no place here for judgment. Every parent reading this is doing their best. Every child struggling deserves to be understood.

Parenting is one of the most demanding and most extraordinary things a human being can do. It asks you to pour yourself into another person completely, without a roadmap, often without warning, and always with everything at stake. I wrote this book because I believe parents deserve better tools — not to be perfect, but to be present, informed, and connected to the children in their care.

My deepest hope is that somewhere in these chapters, you find the clarity you were looking for. That you recognize your child a little more clearly. That you feel a little less alone in the questions that keep you up at night.

You are not failing. You are learning. And so, in the most beautiful way, are they.

Dr. Faisal Ahmed, MD

Board-Certified Child and Adolescent Psychiatrist

California

SPECIAL THANKS

I am deeply grateful to Dr. Ozra Nobari, MD, Dr. Monila Rahimi, DO, and Dr. Robert L. Blanco — board-certified child and adolescent psychiatrists from the greater Sacramento region — for their generous contribution. Each carefully reviewed the manuscript and offered important suggestions and edits that have strengthened the book's clarity, accuracy, and compassion.

I am also thankful to Dr. Amber Haque — a prolific author and research psychologist — for his valuable insights and feedback.

Every parent hopes their child will follow safely — but without early guidance, children can wander into hidden dangers before anyone notices

TABLE OF CONTENTS

CHAPTER ONE

GROWTH AND DEVELOPMENT

Watching Little Ones Blossom into their Best Selves

As a child and adolescent psychiatrist, one lesson has stayed with me throughout my career: you can't understand what's wrong until you understand what's right.

That's exactly what this chapter is about. Before we dive into mental health challenges, we need to understand how children are supposed to grow — physically, emotionally, and mentally. Whether you're a parent tracking your child's milestones, a teacher trying to connect with a struggling student, or an adult reflecting on your own upbringing, this chapter is for you.

We'll draw on some of psychology's greatest thinkers — Freud, Erikson, Piaget, Bowlby — but always in plain language, without the textbook.

It Starts Before Birth

Development begins in the womb. During the second trimester, the brain undergoes rapid growth — neurons multiplying, connections forming at a staggering rate. This is also when the developing brain is most vulnerable to stress, toxins, and poor nutrition. A stable, nurturing environment during pregnancy isn't a luxury — it's a foundation for everything that follows.

Infancy: A World of Pure Wonder (Ages 0–2)

Newborns arrive completely helpless but with enormous purpose behind every cry and every feeding. The brain starts at one-third of adult size and grows to 60% by the end of year one — rapidly building connections based on early experiences.

Three psychology giants each describe this stage a little differently, and together they paint a complete picture:

- Freud called it the oral stage — comfort and connection come primarily through feeding.
- Erikson framed it as trust vs. mistrust — when caregivers respond reliably, babies learn the world is safe and they are loved.

- Piaget called it the sensorimotor stage — babies learn entirely through their senses and physical actions.

Key milestones: Social smiling at 2 months, babbling by 4 months, stranger anxiety around 8–9 months, and separation anxiety peaking between 10 and 18 months. That clinging, crying baby is not being difficult — they're developing exactly as they should.

What This Means for You

Respond consistently. You won't spoil a baby by meeting their needs — you'll build the secure foundation everything else grows on.

The Preschool Years: Imagination Unleashed (Ages 2–5)

Welcome to the age of "why?" and "watch me!" Language explodes, magical thinking takes over, and children become deeply creative. Piaget called this the pre-operational stage — kids this age are egocentric, not because they're selfish, but because their brains genuinely can't yet see the world through someone else's eyes.

Play evolves from parallel play at age 2 (side by side, not quite together) to cooperative play by 3–5 (real teamwork, shared rules). Erikson's initiative vs. guilt describes children who love bold new adventures but also feel genuine guilt when they go too far.

School Age: Building Skills and Finding Your Place (Ages 6–12)

Something shifts around age 6. Children become more logical, goal-oriented, and motivated by accomplishment. Piaget's concrete operations stage brings real cause-and-effect thinking and the ability to consider another person's perspective.

Erikson calls this industry vs. inferiority. Children who experience success build confidence. Those who face repeated failure — especially without support — quietly begin to believe they're not good enough.

Adolescence: The Identity Quest (Ages 12–18+)

Adolescence is where things get turbulent — and for good reason. Puberty arrives with major physical changes. For girls, it typically begins between 8 and 13 with breast development. For boys, between 10 and 14, starting with testicular growth. But the bigger transformation is happening in the brain and the sense of self.

Erikson called this identity vs. role confusion. Teens are asking the biggest question of their young lives: Who am I? They try on different personalities, friend groups, and beliefs — and that's not just normal, it's necessary. Peers become incredibly influential during these years. Your job as a parent is to give them enough space to grow while staying close enough to catch them if they fall.

Attachment: The Glue That Holds Us Together

Of all the concepts in child development, attachment may matter most for long-term mental health. John Bowlby described it as the deep emotional bond between a baby and their primary caregiver — the blueprint for every close relationship that follows.

Mary Ainsworth identified four attachment patterns:

Attachment Style	What It Looks Like
Secure (~60% of children)	Distressed when caregiver leaves, quickly comforted on return. Trusts that support is available.
Anxious / Avoidant	Shows little distress at separation, indifferent at reunion. Has learned not to expect comfort.
Anxious / Resistant	Intensely distressed during separation, hard to soothe even after reunion.
Disorganized	Erratic, contradictory behavior — often linked to trauma or fear.

Secure attachment is one of the strongest predictors of emotional health and resilience throughout life. The good news: insecure attachment isn't a life sentence. With awareness and professional support, those patterns can absolutely change.

Erikson's Eight Stages: A Roadmap for Life

Erikson believed development never stops. Each stage presents a central challenge — master it and you grow; get stuck and it ripples forward.

Stage/Age	Core Challenge
Infancy (0–1)	Trust vs. Mistrust
Toddler (1–3)	Autonomy vs. Shame & Doubt
Preschool (3–6)	Initiative vs. Guilt
School Age (6–12)	Industry vs. Inferiority
Adolescence (12–18)	Identity vs. Role Confusion
Young Adult (18–40)	Intimacy vs. Isolation
Middle Adult (40–65)	Generativity vs. Stagnation

Late Adult (65+)	Integrity vs. Despair

Piaget's Stages: How Kids Learn to Think

Stage	Age Range & Key Feature
Sensorimotor	0–2 years: learning through senses and movement
Pre-Operational	2–7 years: symbolic thinking, egocentrism
Concrete Operational	7–11 years: logical reasoning about concrete objects
Formal Operational	12+ years: abstract and hypothetical thinking

Milestones at a Glance

<u>Gross Motor:</u> Head support (2 months), rolling (4 months), sitting (6 months), crawling and standing (7–12 months), walking (12–18 months), hopping (4 years), catching a ball (4–5 years).

<u>Fine Motor:</u> Reaching (2 months), pincer grasp (8–10 months), stacking blocks (13 months), dressing independently (2–3 years), drawing a circle (3 years), square (4 years), triangle (5 years).

<u>Language:</u> Cooing (2–4 months), first words (12–18 months), two-word phrases (2 years), full sentences (2–3 years). Vocabulary jumps from roughly 50 words at age 2 to 2,000 by age 5.

<u>Emotional</u>: Distress from birth, stranger anxiety around 8 months, separation anxiety peaking at 10–18 months, early embarrassment by 15–24 months, pride and guilt emerging by ages 3–5.

Before We Move On

Development is rarely a straight line. It's messy, nonlinear, and wonderfully unique to each child. What matters most isn't perfection — it's connection, consistency, and the willingness to pay attention. If something feels off, trust that instinct and reach out to a professional. Early support almost always makes a meaningful difference.

Development doesn't stop at 18. Growth remains available at every stage of life — for your child, and for you.

What This Means for You

- Normal development is messy and nonlinear — resist the urge to compare your child to others.
- The most important thing you can give your child in the early years is consistent, responsive care. You cannot spoil a baby by meeting their needs.
- Secure attachment — built through reliable, warm caregiving — is one of the strongest predictors of lifelong emotional health.
- If something feels off with your child's development, trust that instinct. Early support almost always makes a meaningful difference.
- Adolescence is supposed to feel turbulent. Your teenager trying on different identities is not a warning sign — it is exactly what development requires.

CHAPTER TWO

NEURODEVELOPMENTAL DISORDERS

Decoding the Brain's Early Wiring

Now that we understand how the brain is supposed to develop, let's talk about what happens when that development takes a different path from the very beginning.

Neurodevelopmental disorders aren't character flaws, bad parenting, or personal failures. They're conditions rooted in how the brain grows and wires itself — often before a child ever takes their first step or speaks their first word. The goal here isn't to overwhelm you with clinical terms. It's to help you see these conditions with clarity and compassion — because understanding is always the first step toward support.

The Umbrella Concept: Understanding Comorbidity

Think of neurodevelopmental disorders as existing under a single umbrella. Rather than appearing in isolation, multiple diagnoses often exist as entities within that umbrella. Autism spectrum disorder, attention deficit hyperactivity disorder, learning disabilities, intellectual disability, and tic disorders all fall under this broader framework.

Here's what's crucial for parents to understand: neurodevelopmental disorders rarely come alone. They usually come in pairs or multiples. There's a very heavy association between autism spectrum disorder and ADHD. There's a very heavy association between ADHD and learning disorders. In this population, multiple comorbidities are more the rule than the exception.

What This Means for You

For a child with low-functioning autism, learning is critically important — especially speech development and the further learning of basic life skills. Anything that can serve as a hindrance to that process should be addressed very aggressively. That's why early speech therapy is so vital. Additionally, ADHD comorbidity can significantly impact a child's ability to learn new skills. The window of opportunity narrows considerably once a child reaches their teenage years, which is why early identification and intervention are so essential.

Genetics: Why Some Disorders Run in Families

Many neurodevelopmental conditions have a genetic component. Understanding the pattern of inheritance helps families make sense of their history.

- Autosomal Dominant — Only one copy of an altered gene is needed to cause the condition. It affects males and females equally, and a parent who carries it has a 50% chance of passing it to each child.
- Autosomal Recessive — Both parents must carry the gene for a child to be affected. Carriers themselves usually show no symptoms. Each child of two carriers has a 25% chance of being affected.
- X-Linked — The gene is located on the X chromosome. Because males have only one X chromosome, they're more likely to show the full condition.

Genetic testing and counseling can be a powerful tool for families trying to understand their history or plan for the future.

Intellectual Disability: Reframing the Conversation

What was once labeled "Mental Retardation" is now called Intellectual Disability (ID) — a shift in language that reflects a more respectful, strengths-based approach to care. To meet the diagnosis, three things must be present: significant limitations in thinking and reasoning (typically an IQ below 70–75), difficulties with adaptive skills like self-care and social interaction, and onset before age 18.

Severity ranges from Mild (most people can live semi-independently) to Moderate, Severe, and Profound. For children under age 5 with delays across multiple areas, the term Global Developmental Delay is used as a temporary placeholder while assessment continues.

What This Means For You

Early intervention — speech therapy, occupational therapy, educational support — makes an enormous difference. The earlier the support begins, the better the outcomes.

Autism Spectrum Disorder: Understanding the Spectrum

The word "spectrum" matters here. ASD looks dramatically different from person to person — some individuals are nonverbal and require significant daily support, while others are highly verbal, intellectually gifted, and navigating the world with more subtle social challenges.

Modern diagnosis centers on two core areas:

- Social Communication and Interaction — Difficulty with back-and-forth conversation, limited use of eye contact or gestures, and challenges forming and maintaining relationships.
- Restricted and Repetitive Behaviors — At least two of the following: repetitive movements or speech, rigid routines and resistance to change, intense narrow fixations, or unusual sensitivity to sensory experiences.

Treatment focuses on building skills rather than chasing a cure: educational and behavioral therapies, speech and language therapy, and medications when needed for specific symptoms like aggression, anxiety, or attention difficulties. Many people with ASD live rich, meaningful lives.

One pattern I see frequently in my clinic is that children with ASD often develop a significant aversion to school and social situations altogether. The sensory demands, the unpredictability of peers, and the constant expectation to navigate unwritten social rules can make school feel genuinely overwhelming. However, in my clinical opinion, removing a child from school — while it may feel like a relief in the short term — often makes things worse. Withdrawal from the school environment tends to deepen social isolation, erode the routines that many children with ASD depend on, and make reintegration significantly harder over time. The goal should be to adapt the school environment to the child's needs, not to remove the child from it.

The Challenge of High Functioning Autism

The real diagnostic challenge lies with children who have high functioning autism. This presentation is subtle, frequently missed, and often confused with social anxiety disorder or ADHD, with whom it shares considerable symptom overlap. Unlike more visible presentations, these children can form friendships — but tend to gravitate toward others like them, and feel distinctly out of place in broader social settings.

Initiating conversation is genuinely difficult, and reciprocity — the natural back-and-forth of social exchange — is something many struggle with. Their intense, often eccentric interests tend to dominate conversations, gradually causing peers to distance themselves. I see the resulting depression frequently in my practice — often emerging around ages ten to twelve and deepening over time as children begin to internalize their difficulties not as a neurological difference, but as personal failure. Parents should watch for early signs of withdrawal, low mood, and self-critical thinking in this age group.

Sensory sensitivities add further complexity. Many of these children react strongly to sounds, textures, and other input — responding with what looks like aggression or shutting down entirely, reactions often mistaken for behavioral problems. Occupational therapy, noise-canceling headphones, and weighted blankets can make a real difference. Removing these children from school — however well-intentioned — tends to deepen their avoidance rather than resolve it. Structured, supported social engagement remains essential to their development.

Rett Syndrome

Rett syndrome is a rare genetic condition affecting almost exclusively girls, caused by a mutation in the MECP2 gene. It affects roughly 1 in 10,000 to 20,000 girls. Children develop normally in their first year, then gradually lose skills — purposeful hand use, speech, and mobility. Repetitive hand movements, seizures, and breathing irregularities are common. Importantly, emotional awareness is preserved: these children understand and feel far more than they can express, and that should shape how families connect with them. Supportive care through physical therapy, occupational therapy, and communication aids helps maintain quality of life.

There is now real reason for hope. A gene therapy called NGN-401 has received FDA Breakthrough Therapy designation and shown early skill gains in clinical trials — the most significant development in decades. It is not yet widely available, but families can follow progress at rettsyndrome.org.

Genetic Syndromes: A Closer Look

<u>Down Syndrome (Trisomy 21)</u> — The most common genetic cause of intellectual disability. Associated with elevated Alzheimer's risk in adulthood and notable overlap with autism. Early intervention significantly improves outcomes.

<u>Fragile X Syndrome</u> — The second most common genetic cause of intellectual disability. More prevalent in males. Common features include mild to moderate intellectual disability; about 80% of

affected individuals also have ADHD.

Prader-Willi Syndrome — Children are typically short, have low muscle tone, and develop an intense drive to eat that can lead to dangerous obesity without careful management. Mild to moderate intellectual disability is common.

Angelman Syndrome — Children often have a distinctive wide, open-mouthed smile, a puppet-like walking gait, and epilepsy. Most have moderate to severe intellectual disability.

Williams Syndrome — Children often have distinctive "elfin" facial features, heart defects, significant difficulty with visual-spatial tasks, alongside exceptional verbal and musical abilities.

Epilepsy: When the Brain's Electricity Misfires

Epilepsy frequently accompanies neurodevelopmental disorders. A seizure is a single event of abnormal electrical activity in the brain, while epilepsy is defined by recurrent, unprovoked seizures.

Seizures fall into two broad categories: Partial (Focal) Seizures that begin in one area of the brain, and Generalized Seizures that involve the whole brain from the start. The most recognizable types include Tonic-Clonic (grand mal) seizures, brief Absence seizures (staring spells often mistaken for daydreaming), Myoclonic jerks, and Infantile Spasms — a serious type appearing around 6 months requiring prompt treatment. If your child has an unprovoked seizure, seek medical evaluation promptly. Early diagnosis and treatment significantly reduce the risk of further episodes and long-term impact.

Putting It All Together

Neurodevelopmental disorders are complex — but they are not hopeless. Early identification, accurate diagnosis, and consistent support can dramatically change a child's trajectory. The brain is remarkably adaptable, especially in the early years, and the right interventions at the right time make a genuine difference.

If you're a parent with concerns, trust your instincts and pursue evaluation sooner rather than later. These conditions are part of the full spectrum of human experience. The goal isn't to fix people — it's to understand them, support them, and help them build lives that feel meaningful and whole

What This Means for You

- Neurodevelopmental disorders are rooted in brain wiring — not parenting failures or personal shortcomings.
- These conditions rarely travel alone. If your child has one diagnosis, ask the evaluating clinician whether others should be explored.
- The earlier intervention begins, the better. The brain is most adaptable in the early years — act on concerns promptly rather than waiting to see if a child "grows out of it."
- A diagnosis should open doors to support, not define your child's ceiling. Many people with neurodevelopmental conditions live full, rich, and meaningful lives.
- Genetic counseling is available if you have family history concerns and want to understand the inheritance patterns.

CHAPTER THREE

UNPACKING ADHD

It's Not Just "Being Hyper"

ADHD isn't just a label for hyperactivity or scattered moments. It's a legitimate neurological condition wired right into the brain. Brain scans show real differences: areas like the prefrontal cortex and the cerebellum often develop more slowly in people with ADHD. It's biology, not a character flaw.

What ADHD Actually Looks Like

Symptoms fall into two categories: inattention and hyperactivity/impulsivity. Each has nine signs, but six from one (or both) categories are needed for a diagnosis.

<u>Inattention</u> — the "zoned-out" zone: Struggling to stay focused, getting distracted by anything in the environment, forgetting tasks or items, chronic disorganization, avoiding long-attention tasks.

<u>Hyperactivity/Impulsivity</u> — the "can't-stop-won't-stop" side: Constant motion, fidgeting, squirming, rushing through things with errors, excessive talking, interrupting.

ADHD comes in three types: Inattentive (mostly daydreaming), Hyperactive/Impulsive (mostly energetic), or Combined (both worlds). Girls and women often lean inattentive — flying under the radar — while boys and men tend to show more hyperactive traits.

Three Core Brain Challenges

<u>Task Switching:</u> Shifting attention is genuinely hard. When someone with ADHD is deeply focused on something, flipping to something else requires major effort. Parents: if your child is engrossed in a game, polite requests may literally not register. Get eye contact first, then guide gently.

<u>Processing Speed</u>: ADHD can slow how the brain processes inputs. When stimulation is low, the brain generally manages well. When it becomes overwhelming, the system freezes. In kids, overstimulation at a party can spark meltdowns. Offer sensory breaks: "Let's step outside for five minutes."

Impulse Control — The Stop and Go Problem: The brain signals when to act or pause. ADHD can glitch this system under stress, leading to impulsivity or sudden freezes. Strategy: pick your battles. Let minor stuff slide; focus on what really matters.

The Hidden Cost: Emotional Dysregulation

Many children with ADHD don't just struggle academically — they also battle emotional dysregulation, and this is where things get complicated for parents.

Think of ADHD as a battle between two brain systems: the reactive brain and the thinking brain. The thinking brain — mainly the prefrontal cortex — is responsible for planning, decision-making, impulse control, and emotional regulation. When the prefrontal cortex is not functioning efficiently, the reactive brain takes over. This reactive brain is fast, emotional, and survival-focused. It doesn't think; it just reacts.

When this happens, children experience significant frustration. And frustration, left unaddressed, leads to anger and aggression. When we treat ADHD effectively, a lot of these behavioral and emotional symptoms improve significantly — especially aggression.

When a Louder Voice Becomes the Only One That Works

One of the most heartbreaking patterns I see in my clinic is what I call the louder-voice cycle. Parents come in exhausted and frustrated. “He doesn’t listen unless I raise my voice.” “Nothing gets done until I speak louder.” “I hate that it works, but it does.”

I understand. And I want you to know — this is not a parenting failure. It’s a neurology problem that has quietly taken over the household.

Here’s what’s happening beneath the surface. Children with ADHD don’t just struggle with attention and hyperactivity — they also have significant difficulty processing auditory information in real time. A calm instruction delivered across the room registers, at best, as background noise. The brain simply hasn’t flagged it as urgent. It hasn’t broken through.

But a louder, more urgent voice? That changes the stimulus. It’s sudden, it activates the brain’s alert system — and suddenly the child responds. The parent, without meaning to, has learned that speaking louder is the key that works. The pattern gets reinforced on both sides.

A young child who grows up in an environment where calm communication doesn't land — and where an elevated voice is the primary signal that something matters — begins to internalize something deeply troubling: that this is how people communicate when things are serious. They don't learn to self-regulate. They learn to escalate. Meltdowns, outbursts, emotional flooding — these aren't just symptoms of ADHD. In part, they become learned patterns. The child has absorbed the lesson that intensity gets results.

Even more concerning is what the child doesn't understand. Because ADHD interferes with auditory processing and emotional integration, many of these children genuinely cannot explain what they did wrong or why a consequence was given. They weren't choosing to ignore. Their brain simply didn't process the instruction in time. Yet what they experience is repeated frustration, disappointment, and correction — often delivered in an elevated tone. Over time, this shapes how they see themselves: I'm always in trouble. I always get it wrong. No one thinks I'm trying.

This is how ADHD, left unaddressed in the home environment, quietly erodes a child's self-esteem — not through any single dramatic event, but through the daily accumulation of feeling misunderstood. The goal isn't to make parents feel guilty — most families I work with are doing their absolute best under real strain. The goal is to interrupt this cycle before it becomes the family's default language, and before the child decides that loud, reactive communication is simply how the world works.

Treatment: Three Pillars

Biological: Low dopamine is central to ADHD. Medications — mostly stimulants — work by increasing dopamine availability in the brain and are effective for 80–90% of people. One important consideration is rebound syndrome: when medication wears off, many children experience extreme frustration, irritability, and exhaustion. Adjusting medication timing can address this effectively.

Psychological: Therapy for behaviors. People with ADHD are often bright but frustrated, which can lead to depression, anxiety, or aggression. Behavioral plans with rewards and consequences help. Parents benefit from training to respond positively.

Psychosocial: Accommodations make a huge difference — school plans with extra time and quiet testing spaces, organizational apps, structured routines.

What This Means For You

Children with ADHD tend to do much better with visual processing than auditory processing. Calling your child from another room and expecting them to listen probably won't work. Get eye contact first — walk over, make sure you have their attention, then give your instruction. This single shift changes everything.

Practical Strategies that Actually Work

Token Economy and Short-Term Rewards: Children with ADHD respond exceptionally well to short-term, concrete rewards. The key is making the reward immediate and tangible. Don't wait a week; reward today.

Visual Cues for Daily Responsibilities: Post visual reminders of daily chores in your child's room or common areas. Pictures, checklists, or simple written steps work better than verbal reminders.

Timers as Tools: Using timers is highly effective. "You have fifteen minutes to get ready for school" is concrete. The timer becomes the "bad guy," not you. This reduces nagging and clarifies time — something children with ADHD often struggle to conceptualize.

Whether it's you or your child, ADHD is manageable with the right understanding and support.

What This Means for You

- ADHD is a brain-based condition — not laziness, bad attitude, or poor parenting.
- Always get eye contact before giving instructions. Calling from another room rarely works with an ADHD brain.
- Rebound syndrome is real: when medication wears off, behavior can temporarily worsen. Talk to your child's prescriber about timing adjustments.
- Short-term, visible rewards work far better than delayed consequences for children with ADHD. Keep the feedback loop tight.
- Visual schedules and timers reduce daily conflict more than any amount of verbal reminding.
- Untreated ADHD raises long-term risks — including academic failure, low self-esteem, and substance use. Early treatment protects your child's future.

CHAPTER FOUR

ANXIETY IN KIDS

It's More Than Just Butterflies

Anxiety disorders affect approximately 1 in 8 to 1 in 5 children and adolescents in the U.S., with rates higher in teens — up to 16–20% currently diagnosed in recent surveys. That's a significant number of children and their families navigating this daily. Anxiety isn't just "nerves" or overthinking — it's a real disorder that can hijack a kid's world. The good news? It's highly treatable, and many kids do remarkably well with the right support.

The Main Types of Anxiety Disorders

Separation Anxiety Disorder: Especially common in younger children. An intense, paralyzing fear of abandonment or harm to loved ones — clinging at drop-off, nightmares about losing you, or outright school refusal.

Social Anxiety Disorder: Social situations feel like being under a spotlight of judgment. Kids dread being scrutinized, so they avoid parties, group activities, or even raising a hand in class. This isn't shyness — it's a deep fear of embarrassment that genuinely limits daily life.

Panic Disorder: Panic attacks are intense, brief episodes — typically 10–15 minutes — marked by a racing heart, chest pain, dizziness, sweating, and nausea. Children often describe feeling like they're dying or losing control.

Generalized Anxiety Disorder (GAD): The "worry about everything" presentation — persistent concern about school, friends, health, and the future, accompanied by physical symptoms like fatigue, restlessness, muscle tension, and sleep trouble.

A Note on OCD and PTSD: The DSM-5 no longer classifies either OCD or PTSD under the anxiety disorders category — each now has its own distinct classification. That said, both conditions carry a heavy burden of anxiety and can present with significant disability in children and adolescents. Early evaluation and treatment make a meaningful difference.

Where Does Anxiety Come From?

It's a classic nature-nurture mix. Genes play a role — if anxiety runs in the family, kids are more prone. Environmentally, overprotective parenting that stifles exploration, or consistent lack of emotional validation, can amplify anxiety over time. Children crave affirmation; without it, they can grow indecisive and chronically worried.

When Helping Feels Right but Backfires

This is one of the hardest things to say to a loving parent — but it needs to be said: sometimes the very way parents try to help their anxious child ends up making things significantly worse.

When a child is anxious, the natural parental instinct is to protect. But when protection becomes accommodation — when the environment is consistently reshaped around a child's anxiety rather than helping the child build tolerance for it — we unintentionally teach the child that the world truly is too dangerous to face.

One of the most common patterns is school avoidance. Removing a child from school doesn't resolve the anxiety; it confirms it. The message the anxious brain receives is: you were right to be afraid, and the only way to feel safe is to avoid. Each time a child escapes an anxiety-provoking situation, the relief powerfully reinforces the avoidance — and the anxiety digs in deeper.

What This Means for You

The clinical term for this pattern is accommodation — and research consistently shows that high levels of parental accommodation are associated with more severe and persistent anxiety in children. This is not about blame. Parents who accommodate are not doing something wrong intentionally; they are doing what feels humane. But treating childhood anxiety effectively means helping families understand that tolerating short-term discomfort, with proper support, is how children build long-term resilience.

How I Address School Refusal: Gradual Desensitization

When school refusal emerges, I use a structured approach grounded in cognitive behavioral therapy principles called gradual desensitization. Rather than forcing full-time attendance immediately or allowing complete avoidance, we meet the child where they are and build tolerance incrementally.

Typically, I collaborate with the school to allow the child to attend for just two hours a day — perhaps mornings only — for one to two weeks. Once they've acclimated, we extend to three hours, then four, and so on. The process usually takes two to four weeks total. By the end, the child has been gradually desensitized to the full school environment and can integrate back into regular attendance. This approach requires close coordination with the school — most are willing to accommodate when the clinical rationale is clearly communicated.

Treatment: What Actually Works

Before any diagnosis is made, it is worth ruling out medical causes — anemia, hyperthyroidism, and other conditions can produce symptoms that closely resemble anxiety. Then assess severity:

- Mild (worries but functioning well) — therapy first.
- Moderate (some avoidance, partial dysfunction) — therapy, with medication added if needed.
- Severe (unable to leave home, complete school shutdown) — often requires both, started simultaneously.

Medications: SSRIs like sertraline (Zoloft) or fluoxetine (Prozac) are FDA-approved for children and generally well-tolerated. SNRIs address both anxiety and depression when both are present.

Cognitive Behavioral Therapy (CBT): The gold standard. CBT helps children identify distorted thinking patterns — black-and-white thinking, catastrophizing, magnifying negatives — and learn to challenge and restructure them.

What the Research Tells Us: The CAMS Study

The Child/Adolescent Anxiety Multimodal Study (CAMS) enrolled 488 children and adolescents between ages 7 and 17 with separation anxiety disorder, generalized anxiety disorder, or social phobia. They were divided into four groups: medication alone (sertraline), CBT alone, the combination of both, and placebo.

The results were clear: combination treatment showed the strongest acute response (approximately 81%), outperforming both individual treatments. The majority of children who responded to active treatments maintained meaningful improvements in longer-term follow-up. Over 80% of acute responders held onto their gains, and the combination group showed the most durable benefit.

The clinical takeaway: medication can provide faster initial relief, CBT builds skills that protect against relapse, and combining the two gives children the best chance at both rapid improvement and lasting recovery.

What This Means for You

- Anxiety disorders are among the most common — and most treatable — conditions in childhood. Getting help early makes a real difference.
- Helping your child avoid everything they fear makes anxiety worse over time, not better. Gradual, supported exposure is the path through.
- School refusal is a clinical emergency, not a phase to wait out. Involve a mental health professional promptly.
- If you recognize that your responses may be accommodating your child's anxiety, don't feel guilty — seek a clinician who can help the whole family recalibrate.
- For moderate to severe anxiety, combining medication with CBT produces the strongest and most lasting results.
- Watch for physical symptoms — stomachaches, headaches, and fatigue in children are often anxiety presenting in disguise.

CHAPTER FIVE

THE MULTIPLE FACES OF CHILDHOOD TRAUMA

Healing from the Shadows

Two Patients I Have Never Forgotten

Early in my training, I encountered two patients who have stayed with me ever since — not because they were unusual, but because they were not. I have seen versions of them many times since. And every time I do, the same question returns.

The first was a 26-year-old man, referred for a pretrial psychiatric evaluation after being charged with burglary. His chart read like a map of compounding failures: repeated criminal offenses, multiple prison terms, and a childhood marked by ADHD, conduct disorder, and oppositional defiant disorder. His father was an alcoholic who was episodically violent. His mother worked long hours to support the family and was rarely home. As a child, he had been evaluated and briefly treated at a community mental health center after being caught setting fire to an abandoned warehouse. His teachers described him as fidgety, restless, and persistently disruptive. Through adolescence, a school psychologist worked with him for a consistent pattern of antisocial behavior — car theft, joyriding, drunk driving, driving on a suspended license, and stealing money from his mother. He had no close friendships, yet was a powerful and respected member of a hot rod gang — the closest thing to belonging he had ever known. He was sexually active from an early age and took pride in it, yet remained deeply mistrustful of women and grew easily bored with the same partner. By his mid-twenties he had abandoned his wife on suspicions of infidelity. Eight months later, he was arrested again.

The second was a 19-year-old young woman I saw during my fellowship, referred by her primary care physician for depression. What I noticed first, before she said a word, were the cigarette burns — six on her left arm, three on her right — and the razor marks. She had recently lost her job due to irritability and erratic behavior. Her parents had divorced when she was 18 months old, and she had never known her father. She had been sexually abused by her mother's boyfriend from ages six to eight. She did well in school until third grade, then slowly stopped trying, and dropped out in eleventh grade. By the time I met her, she had been living with chronic suicidal ideation for three years, burning and cutting herself intermittently as a form of self-punishment — stopping, she told me, only when she felt she had suffered enough. She described shifting from intense crying into hysterical laughter without warning. She carried a profound sense of worthlessness and had come to accept chronic emptiness as simply her fate.

I always find myself wondering: would I have been seeing either of these patients in these settings if they had not grown up in such chaos? That question still stays with me. I believe deeply in biological illness — genetics, neurochemistry, brain development all matter. But I am never able to stop asking how much of what I was witnessing in both of these people was trauma, moving quietly underneath every diagnosis on the page.

In the U.S., over 4 million children face trauma yearly, increasing risks for mental health issues, conduct problems, and disrupted development. But with the right understanding and support, healing is genuinely possible.

How Children Experience Trauma Differently

Children do not perceive or process trauma the way adults do. In my clinical experience, trauma affects children differently depending on their age and developmental stage — and in most cases, children do not process it as efficiently as adults. Instead, it sits quietly in the background, stored in the subconscious, shaping how they see the world long before they have words to describe it.

The most profound effect I observe is a fundamental shift in the child's relationship with their environment: a loss of basic trust. Every healthy, growing child carries an innate assumption — a kind of quiet confidence — that the world is safe until proven otherwise. That baseline is what allows children to explore, take risks, form relationships, and learn. Trauma replaces that baseline with its opposite: the constant, unshakeable sense that something bad is going to happen.

I think of it like a car with a misaligned steering system. The default of a well-functioning car is to drive straight — you only turn the wheel when you need to. In the same way, the default of a healthy human being is to trust the environment, to assume stability. Trauma misaligns that system. These children are never driving straight. They are constantly bracing, scanning, correcting. Even in safe, stable situations, they cannot fully relax into the present moment. There is always an undercurrent of fear that things will not last — that the calm is temporary, that something is about to fall apart.

Trauma misaligns the brain's default setting — these children are never driving straight, always scanning for the next impact

This hypervigilance doesn't simply fade as the child grows. It follows them into adulthood. Even as adults, survivors of childhood trauma often find themselves constantly trying to convince themselves that things are okay — even when they objectively are. The environment may be safe, the relationship stable, the circumstances good — and yet the underlying fear persists. This is why unresolved childhood trauma has such a powerful effect on adult relationships: the foundation of trust, which should form naturally in early childhood, was never allowed to set.

A Child Who Could Only Show What He Could Not Say

I want to share a clinical encounter from my child psychiatry fellowship that has stayed with me ever since — one that taught me more about how children carry trauma than any textbook could.

I was evaluating a six-year-old boy alongside my mentor, the late Dr. Arshad Hussain, a child psychiatrist whose wisdom shaped my entire approach to this work. God bless his soul. The child came in appearing extremely hyperactive — unable to sit still, constantly in motion, with poor eye contact and what seemed like a very short attention span. Our initial clinical impression leaned toward ADHD and possibly autism spectrum disorder.

Dr. Hussain, with his characteristic gentleness and intuition, handed the child a piece of paper and asked him to draw. The boy, who had been difficult to engage verbally, took to it immediately. He drew a house with five windows — and colored one of them completely black.

When we gently asked him about the black window, he became guarded and still. Then, quietly, he said: "Bad things happen in that room."

In that moment, everything shifted. What had looked like hyperactivity, inattention, and social withdrawal — what we had been prepared to diagnose as ADHD and ASD — was in fact the presentation of a child carrying a significant traumatic burden. He wasn't neurodevelopmentally disordered. He was terrified. And the only language available to him was a crayon and a piece of paper.

This is the lesson I carry from that encounter: children will tell us what they cannot say, if we give them the right way to express it. As clinicians — and as parents — our job is to stay curious, stay patient, and never assume the first diagnosis is the whole story.

Trauma's Ties to Mental Health

Childhood abuse — physical, sexual, or emotional — links directly to adult challenges including mood disorders, anxiety, substance use disorders, and personality disorders. Psychologically, abused children come to see the world as unpredictable and dangerous, and adults as threatening — which can turn them hostile, avoidant, or volatile.

Common patterns that emerge from childhood trauma include: expecting harm even in safe situations, difficulty trusting closeness, feeling powerless, emotionally numbing to survive, misreading others' intentions, and defaulting to aggression when threatened.

The Brain's Battle: Neurobiology of Trauma

Early maltreatment physically changes the developing brain. Neuroimaging studies show smaller amygdala, hippocampus, and key connecting structures in people who experienced childhood trauma. Chronic stress during critical developmental periods floods the brain with stress hormones, reshaping neural systems. The result: the body remains on high alert long after the danger has passed — a survival adaptation that becomes a psychological burden. For parents, this means that a child's behavioral reactions to stress are not simply choices — they are the nervous system responding exactly as it was shaped to respond.

Disorders That Can Develop

<u>PTSD</u>: Children with PTSD have 2–12 times higher risk for depression, substance abuse, and suicidality. Symptoms include re-experiencing trauma

through flashbacks and nightmares, avoidance of reminders, and chronic hyperarousal. When the perpetrator is a family member, symptoms tend to be more severe due to betrayal and self-blame.

Bipolar Disorder and Trauma: About 16% of people with bipolar disorder also have PTSD — double the general population rate. Early trauma seems to prime the brain for mood instability.

Personality Disorders: Trauma is strongly linked to both Antisocial and Borderline Personality Disorders. Physical abuse correlates with antisocial patterns; neglect links to borderline, avoidant, and narcissistic traits.

ADHD and Trauma: A 23–35% overlap exists between ADHD and trauma survivors. Critically, trauma can cause ADHD-like profiles — inattention, fidgeting, reactivity — leading to misdiagnosis. Routine trauma screening for children with apparent ADHD symptoms is essential.

Healing Is Possible

Childhood trauma's scars run deep, but they are not permanent. Effective treatments include EMDR (Eye Movement Desensitization and Reprocessing) for PTSD, DBT (Dialectical Behavior Therapy) for emotional dysregulation, and Trauma-Focused Cognitive Behavioral Therapy (TF-CBT). Support groups and resilience-building programs help rebuild a sense of safety and connection.

What This Means for You

- Childhood trauma physically changes the developing brain — this is not weakness or drama; it is biology.
- Trauma can look like ADHD, conduct problems, or mood disorders. Always ask about a child's history before assuming a behavioral diagnosis.
- A predictable, safe, and warm home environment is itself a powerful form of trauma treatment.
- If your child has experienced trauma, look for a therapist specifically trained in trauma-focused approaches such as TF-CBT (Trauma-Focused Cognitive Behavioral Therapy) or EMDR (Eye Movement Desensitization and Reprocessing).
- Adults who experienced childhood trauma: healing is genuinely possible at any age. The scars do not have to define the story.

CHAPTER SIX

AGGRESSION IN CHILDREN

Understanding and Taming the Storm

Aggression in children is one of the most alarming things a parent can witness — and one of the most misunderstood. It is rarely about a "bad kid" or a character flaw. More often, it is a signal of something deeper: unmet needs, an overwhelmed nervous system, or an underlying condition that has not yet been identified.

Two Types of Aggression

Reactive Aggression: A hot-headed response to perceived threats or frustration — anger flares, tantrums, or vengeful acts. This type is strongly tied to anxiety, mood disorders, ADHD, and impulse control problems.

Proactive Aggression: Cooler and goal-driven — bullying, domination, teasing to gain power or status. Less emotional reactivity, more calculation. This type links more strongly to antisocial traits.

The Brain Behind the Behavior

Aggression is brain-based. Research shows smaller amygdala volumes in youth with persistent aggression. The prefrontal cortex recruits less effectively in aggressive teens, leading to impulse control failures under stress. Key risk factors include family chaos, bullying exposure, co-occurring anxiety or depression, trauma, and ADHD.

Finding the Root Cause

One of the most important things a parent can do when facing aggression in their child is ask not just what is happening, but why. In my clinical experience, aggression rarely exists in a vacuum — it is almost always downstream of something else.

A child with unmedicated ADHD is navigating a world that constantly overwhelms their capacity for focus and impulse control. When the demands exceed what their brain can manage, aggression becomes the pressure valve. Similarly, children on the autism spectrum often carry a significant burden of anxiety that, when it builds without an outlet, can manifest as explosive behavior. This is why identifying and treating the underlying condition is not just helpful — it is essential. Addressing aggression without addressing the ADHD, anxiety, or autism driving it is like treating a fever without looking for the infection.

De-Escalation in the Moment

For ADHD-driven aggression: calm and direct physical presence matters. Get down to the child's eye level, make gentle eye contact, and speak in a slow and steady voice. Remove them from highly stimulating environments and reassure them they are not in trouble.

For anxiety-driven aggression: again, reduce environmental stimulation. Give the child time and space to de-escalate on their own terms. Resist the urge to immediately process what happened. Reassurance, not interrogation, is what the child needs in that moment. A calm, quiet presence from a trusted adult is often the most powerful intervention available.

Building Long-Term Regulation: Token Economy

One of the most effective tools available to parents is a structured token economy combined with a reward system. Children earn tokens for demonstrating controlled behavior in situations that would previously have triggered aggression. Those tokens are then exchanged for agreed-upon rewards.

This approach works best when the expectations are clear, the rewards are meaningful to the child, and the system is applied consistently across settings — home, school, and wherever else the child spends significant time. Involving teachers and other caregivers in the plan is essential.

Treatment

Psychotherapy: Parent Management Training (PMT) teaches prosocial reinforcement strategies. Multisystemic Therapy (MST) cuts reoffending by 30% in trials. Anger management and functional family therapy show meaningful improvements.

Medications: For ADHD-driven aggression, stimulants reduce aggression 40–50%. For mood and anxiety, SSRIs improve reactive aggression by about 35%. For autism-related irritability, risperidone and aripiprazole are FDA-approved.

What This Means for You

- Aggression in children is almost always a symptom of something else — anxiety, ADHD, autism, trauma, or a mood disorder. Look for the "why" before addressing the behavior alone.
- In the moment: get to eye level, speak slowly and calmly, and remove your child from overwhelming environments. Don't escalate.
- Once the storm passes, don't interrogate — reconnect. Processing can happen later, when the nervous system has settled.
- A token economy with immediate, visible rewards is one of the most effective tools for building self-regulation over time.
- Seek a thorough evaluation if aggressive patterns persist. The right diagnosis changes everything about how you respond.

CHAPTER SEVEN

DISRUPTIVE, IMPULSE-CONTROL, AND CONDUCT DISORDERS

Mastering the Urges

These aren't "bad kids" or "flawed characters" — they're often brain-based struggles amplified by life stresses. With early understanding and targeted support, many young people turn these storms into genuine strengths.

Oppositional Defiant Disorder (ODD)

ODD involves a pattern of angry or irritable moods, argumentative or defiant behavior, or vindictiveness lasting at least 6 months, causing real distress or impairment. Four or more specific behaviors must be present, including losing temper easily, arguing with authority figures, actively defying rules, and deliberate vindictiveness.

ODD affects about 3–5% of children. About 67% of cases remit by adulthood with appropriate treatment. Poor prognosis factors include very early onset and co-occurring ADHD, which triples the risk of progressing to Conduct Disorder.

Conduct Disorder (CD): The Rule-Breaker's Path

CD involves repetitive violations of the rights of others or major social norms. Diagnosis requires at least 3 of 15 specific behaviors in the past 12 months — including aggression toward people or animals, destruction of property, deceit or theft, and serious rule violations.

Prevalence is 1.5–3.4%, peaking in late childhood and early teens. Boys outnumber girls 5:1 in diagnosis, though girls' conduct disorder is often more covert. Early onset (before age 10) and the "limited prosocial emotions" specifier indicate more serious long-term risk.

Intermittent Explosive Disorder (IED): Sudden Sparks

IED involves recurrent aggressive outbursts that are grossly out of proportion to the trigger. The pattern is predictable: tension builds, the outburst provides temporary relief, guilt follows. It's not premeditated; it's an impulse control failure. Age 6+ is the minimum for diagnosis.

Pyromania and Kleptomania

While rare, pyromania and kleptomania do present in children and adolescents, and parents who notice these patterns should seek professional evaluation promptly rather than attributing them to curiosity or habit. Pyromania involves deliberate, repeated firesetting with tension before and fascination and relief during — not done for profit or ideology. It's rare, with 40% of arson arrests involving those under 18, and strongly linked to trauma and impulsivity.

Kleptomania involves irresistible urges to steal items that aren't needed — the act is about the tension and release, not the object. It's more common in women (about two-thirds of cases) and has a 60% overlap with other conditions.

Treatment

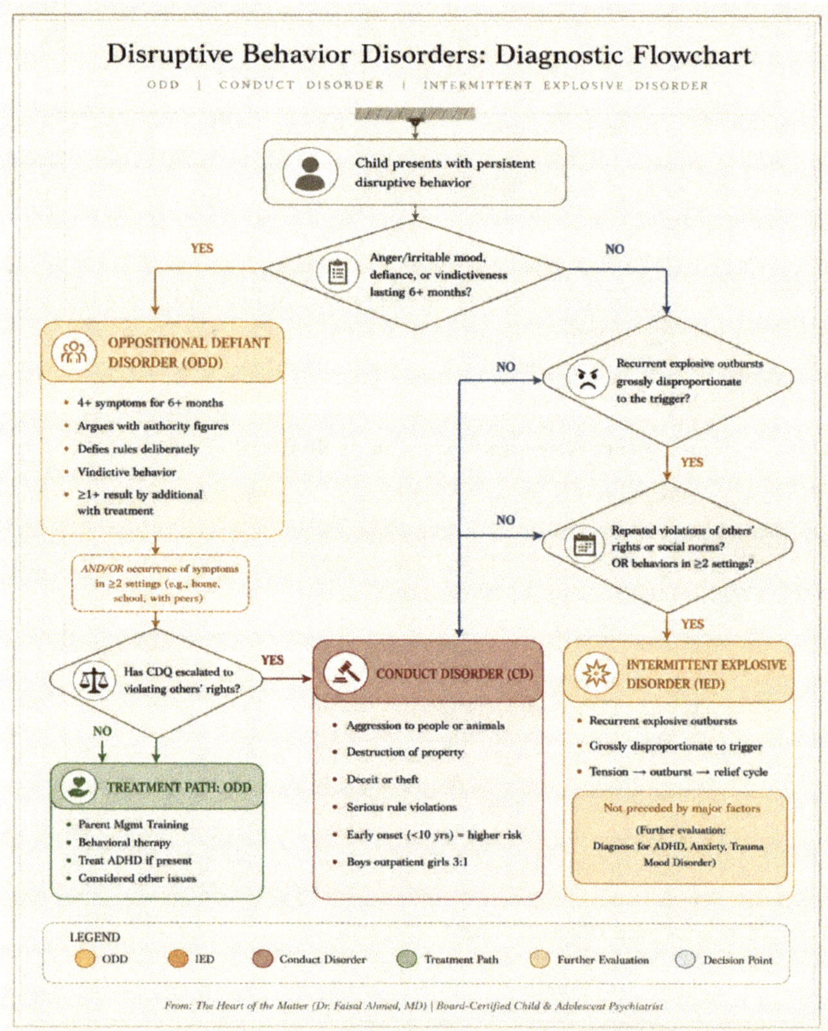

Psychosocial interventions come first. Parent Management Training (PMT) shows moderate reductions in aggression. Multisystemic Therapy (MST) cuts reoffending by 30%. Anger management and functional family therapy show meaningful improvements.

Medications target specific symptoms: stimulants for ADHD-related aggression, SSRIs for reactive aggression and mood, antipsychotics for severe irritability, and mood stabilizers for bipolar-related conduct problems. Combinations of therapy and targeted medications consistently outperform either approach alone.

What This Means for You

- ODD, CD, and related disorders are not character problems — they are treatable conditions with real biological and environmental roots.
- 67% of ODD cases remit by adulthood with appropriate treatment. Early help genuinely changes the trajectory.
- Co-occurring ADHD triples the risk of ODD progressing to Conduct Disorder — treating the ADHD is often the most important first step.
- Behavioral therapy should always come before medication. When medication is added, it targets a specific symptom, not "bad behavior" in general.
- Consistency at home is one of the most powerful tools available. Mixed or unpredictable responses to behavior make these conditions significantly harder to treat.

CHAPTER EIGHT

BIPOLAR DISORDER IN CHILDREN AND ADOLESCENTS

Riding the Emotional Waves

Bipolar disorder in kids and teens is often tricky because it doesn't always look "classic" like it does in adults. Bipolar isn't a "character flaw" or "just hormones" — it's a brain-based condition with genetic and environmental roots. With early detection and tailored care, many people lead stable, fulfilling lives.

How It Looks Different in Young People

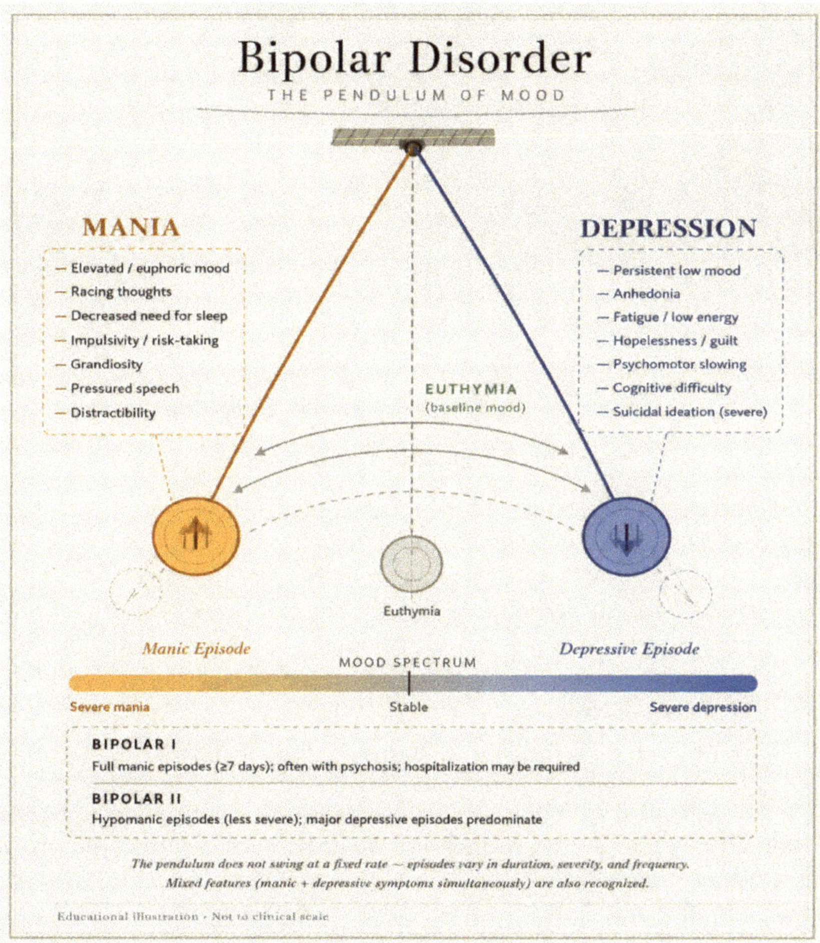

In youth, bipolar often shows up as rapid mood flips, irritability more often than euphoria, and frequent co-occurrence with ADHD or anxiety. Lifetime prevalence of bipolar disorder in adolescents is estimated at around 1–3% when including spectrum conditions, though strict bipolar I is rarer — approximately 0.5–1%. Classic manic highs do occur, but more often in children it's atypical — brief explosive outbursts or chronic, severe irritability.

The same child through two windows — the weight of a depressive episode on the left, the lightness of recovery on the right

The Diagnostic Landscape

DSM-5 sharpened criteria to reduce overdiagnosis. For a manic episode, at least 7 days of elevated or irritable mood must be accompanied by increased energy — a key addition that helps distinguish bipolar from ADHD. Children with chronic irritability and severe emotional outbursts (but no distinct manic episodes) are more accurately diagnosed with Disruptive Mood Dysregulation Disorder (DMDD) — a newer diagnosis that reduced bipolar misdiagnosis by 50%.

Bipolar and Trauma: A Critical Link

About 16–20% of people with bipolar disorder also have PTSD — double the general population rate. Childhood maltreatment increases bipolar risk by 2.6 times, with earlier onset. Effects include more frequent mood episodes, higher suicidality, rapid cycling, and greater stress sensitivity. If trauma is part of the story, integrated care combining trauma-focused therapy with mood management is essential.

Treatment: A Tailored Toolkit

Medications: Lithium remains a cornerstone treatment. Valproate (Depakote) shows similar efficacy, particularly for mixed mood states. Atypical antipsychotics are effective for acute mania (50–70% remission rates). Lurasidone has received approval for pediatric bipolar depression (ages 10+).

Psychotherapy: Medication alone is never enough. Family-Focused Therapy (FFT) has been shown to reduce mood episodes by approximately 40% in clinical trials. Interpersonal and Social Rhythm Therapy (IPSRT) — which focuses on stabilizing daily routines — reduces relapse by about 30%. Psychoeducation for the whole family is essential.

What This Means for You

- Bipolar disorder in children often looks different from adults — irritability and explosive outbursts are more common than classic euphoria.
- If your child has chronic, severe irritability without clear manic episodes, ask about DMDD — it may be a more accurate diagnosis.
- Trauma history significantly worsens bipolar outcomes. If both are present, integrated treatment addressing both is essential.
- Mood tracking is one of the most useful things a family can do — a simple daily log of mood, sleep, and energy helps clinicians see patterns that are invisible in a single appointment.
- Medication alone is never enough. Family therapy and daily routine stability are just as important as the prescription.

CHAPTER NINE

PSYCHOTIC DISORDERS IN CHILDREN

Navigating the Shadows of the Young Mind

Psychosis in children is often misunderstood but crucial for early intervention. These aren't "crazy" children; they're often bright souls overwhelmed by brain-based disruptions, and with the right support, many lead fulfilling lives.

What Is Psychosis?

Psychosis is a loss of touch with reality — a breakdown in the brain's ability to accurately test and interpret the world. Two concepts are essential:

Delusions are fixed, false beliefs held with absolute certainty, even when evidence clearly contradicts them. A child might be convinced that someone is poisoning their food, or that strangers are secretly watching them.

Hallucinations are perceptual disturbances — seeing, hearing, smelling, or feeling things that are not actually there. They feel completely real to the person experiencing them. Hearing voices is the most common form in children.

Psychosis in Children Is Not the Same as in Adults

Development plays an enormous role. A three-year-old who insists there is a monster in the closet is displaying developmentally expected magical thinking. A fifteen-year-old who regularly hears voices telling them what to do is a fundamentally different situation. The key clinical question is always: Is this appropriate for where this child is developmentally, or does it represent a true break from reality?

A Growing Concern: Cannabis and Psychosis

One trend that cannot be ignored is the growing link between cannabis use and psychotic symptoms in young people. Today's cannabis products are significantly more potent than those of previous generations, and the developing adolescent brain is particularly vulnerable. Cannabis-induced psychosis is not rare. For some young people, what begins as recreational use can trigger a psychotic episode that persists well beyond the period of intoxication. This is a conversation parents and clinicians must be willing to have openly.

The Differential Diagnosis: Ruling Out Other Causes

Psychosis in children is not automatically schizophrenia. A careful clinician rules out a wide range of other causes:

- Delirium — Acute confusion from infections, drug intoxication, or metabolic problems.
- Substance or Medication-Induced Psychosis — Corticosteroids, stimulants, and cannabis can all trigger psychotic symptoms.
- Medical Conditions — Brain tumors, autoimmune diseases like lupus, or metabolic disorders.
- Primary Psychosis — When all other causes have been thoroughly ruled out.

How Common Is This?

A large proportion of first schizophrenia episodes emerge during adolescence, with peak onset in the late teens and early twenties. Very Early Onset schizophrenia (before age 13) is rare — accounting for roughly 2% of all schizophrenia cases. For schizophrenia specifically, long-term outcomes vary widely and depend heavily on how early treatment begins, the level of family support, and whether co-occurring conditions are addressed. This is precisely why early identification matters so much.

Treatment: A Multi-Pronged Approach

Medications: Atypical antipsychotics are generally the first choice. FDA-approved options for children include aripiprazole, olanzapine, quetiapine, and risperidone. Weight gain and metabolic changes require regular monitoring.

Psychosocial Interventions: Psychosocial support includes family education and therapy, social skills training, and relapse prevention planning. CBT, special education accommodations, and treatment of any co-occurring conditions are equally important components of care.

What This Means for You

- Trust your instincts. You know your child. If you notice unusual behaviors, social withdrawal, bizarre statements, sensory complaints, or a personality shift that doesn't feel right — those observations matter. The gap between symptom onset and first treatment is one of the strongest predictors of long-term outcome. The shorter that gap, the better.
- A young child insisting there's a monster in the closet is normal. A teenager regularly hearing voices is not — seek evaluation promptly.
- Psychosis is not always schizophrenia. Many causes are treatable and reversible — a thorough medical workup is always the first step.
- Heavy cannabis use can trigger psychosis in adolescents. This is not a rare edge case — it is something I see regularly in clinical practice.
- Children do not always report what they are experiencing. Watch for personality shifts, social withdrawal, or fearfulness that seems disconnected from reality.
- The earlier treatment begins, the better the long-term outcome. Do not wait and watch with psychotic symptoms.

CHAPTER TEN

BORDERLINE PERSONALITY DISORDER

Understanding Intensity, Instability, and the Path to Stability

Borderline Personality Disorder (BPD) is one of the most misunderstood diagnoses in psychiatry. It's also one of the most treatable — with the right support, consistency, and evidence-based therapy, people with BPD build genuinely stable lives.

What Is Borderline Personality Disorder?

BPD is defined by a pervasive pattern of instability in interpersonal relationships, self-image, and emotions, combined with marked impulsivity. To meet diagnostic criteria, a person must show five or more of these nine features:

- Frantic efforts to avoid real or imagined abandonment
- A pattern of unstable relationships that swing between idealization and devaluation
- Identity disturbance with a persistently unstable self-image
- Impulsivity in at least two self-damaging areas (spending, substance use, reckless driving, binge eating)
- Recurrent suicidal behavior, self-harm, or threats
- Affective instability — rapid mood shifts within hours
- Chronic feelings of emptiness
- Inappropriate, intense anger or difficulty controlling it
- Stress-triggered paranoia or dissociative episodes

A Critical Shift: BPD in Adolescents

Historically, personality disorders were not diagnosed before age 18. Current DSM-5-TR criteria have evolved: BPD can now be diagnosed in children and adolescents if the disturbance is pervasive across multiple settings, persistent for at least one year, and not limited to a developmental stage. This shift reflects decades of research showing that BPD can be reliably identified in adolescents as young as 11 years

— and that early recognition changes outcomes dramatically.

The Parent Question: "Attention-Seeking" Behavior

Here's what I hear from parents constantly: "My child has wild mood swings and gets upset over nothing. They just need attention." My question back is always this: Why does this child need so much attention? Isn't that itself a problem worth understanding?

That question shifts everything. Rapid irritability, intense emotional reactions, and urgent bids for reassurance aren't character flaws — they're signals of genuine distress. A child with emerging BPD isn't being difficult; they're struggling with emotions they can't regulate and a sense of self that feels fragmented.

Treatment: Consistency and Early DBT

The hallmark of effective treatment for BPD in adolescents is two-fold: parental consistency and Dialectical Behavior Therapy (DBT).

DBT, developed by psychologist Marsha Linehan, is the gold standard and has the strongest evidence base for BPD. DBT teaches four core skill sets:

- Mindfulness — present-moment awareness without judgment
- Distress Tolerance — surviving crisis without making it worse
- Emotion Regulation — understanding and managing intense feelings
- Interpersonal Effectiveness — communicating needs and boundaries respectfully

Parental consistency is equally critical: validate emotions without reinforcing chaos, establish clear and predictable boundaries, and show up the same way day after day, even when your child pushes you away.

Hope and Reality

Recovery from BPD is not just possible — research consistently shows that many people with BPD see significant improvement over time, particularly with early intervention. Personality disorders are not life sentences. With early recognition, DBT, and consistent parental support, people build stable relationships, manage emotions, and construct meaningful lives. The intensity that once felt like chaos can become a strength — deep feeling, fierce loyalty, and a genuine capacity for connection.

What This Means for You

- "Attention-seeking" is not a character flaw — it is a signal that a child is struggling with emotions they cannot regulate on their own.
- BPD can now be diagnosed in adolescents as young as 11. Early recognition means earlier treatment and better outcomes.
- DBT (Dialectical Behavior Therapy) is the gold standard. If your teen is in therapy but not receiving DBT, ask specifically about it.
- Your consistency as a parent is itself a form of treatment. Showing up the same way every day — even when pushed away — directly counters the fear of abandonment at the core of BPD.
- Validate emotions without reinforcing chaos: "I can see you're in real pain" is different from reshaping the household around every emotional storm.

CHAPTER ELEVEN

EATING DISORDERS: BEYOND THE MIRROR

When Food Becomes the Enemy

Eating disorders aren't just about food. They're tangled up in emotions, self-worth, and sometimes family dynamics. These conditions are on the rise, especially among teenage girls and young women, and they often run in families. Many hide it from loved ones, making these disorders sneaky and dangerous — sometimes fatal if untreated.

The Three Main Types

Anorexia Nervosa: Skipping meals, eating tiny portions of "safe" foods, obsessive calorie-counting, and exercising excessively. The core is an intense, persistent fear of weight gain — even when the person is dangerously underweight.

Bulimia Nervosa: The binge-purge cycle — massive food binges followed by purging through vomiting, laxatives, or extreme exercise, driven by terror of gaining weight. It often happens in secret, leaving the person exhausted and ashamed.

Binge-Eating Disorder: Frequent, out-of-control overeating episodes, often alone and very fast, even when not hungry — but without purging. Followed by waves of guilt and shame. Unlike the others, it affects men and women about equally.

In the U.S., up to 10 in 100 young women deal with an eating disorder. Anorexia and bulimia predominantly affect females, with onset most common between ages 12 and 25, though rates of eating disorders overall are rising across all genders.

Treatment

Anorexia: Restore healthy weight (sometimes with hospitalization if severe), address psychological roots like perfectionism or low self-esteem, and build new, healthier thinking patterns. Family-Based Therapy (FBT) stands out for younger cases — parents take an active role in rebuilding healthy eating habits.

Bulimia: Nutritional counseling, CBT to overhaul the binge-purge cycle, and medications if depression or anxiety are present. Fluoxetine (Prozac) is FDA-approved for bulimia.

Binge-Eating: CBT to manage compulsions, nutritional guidance, and sometimes antidepressants to handle emotional triggers. Breaking the shame cycle is essential.

Eating disorders are serious — but they are absolutely treatable. Early intervention dramatically improves outcomes. Recovery is not just possible; it is common with the right team in place.

What This Means for You

- Eating disorders are not about vanity or food — they are complex psychiatric conditions driven by emotion, self-worth, and often family dynamics.
- Warning signs to watch for: bathroom trips after meals, hidden food wrappers, obsessive calorie counting, excessive exercise, and dramatic weight loss.
- Denial is part of the disorder. A child insisting nothing is wrong does not mean nothing is wrong.
- Family-Based Therapy (FBT) is particularly effective for younger patients — parents play an active role in rebuilding healthy eating, and that involvement matters.
- Treatment requires a team: a physician to monitor physical health, a therapist for the psychological roots, and a nutritionist to rebuild a healthy relationship with food.

CHAPTER TWELVE

THE SCARRED SOUL

Understanding Self-Injury in Teens

Self-injury isn't about "attention-seeking" or weakness; it's often a cry from a scarred soul trying to cope. We'll approach it with care and zero judgment.

The Teen Psyche: A Storm of Changes

Adolescence is a period of profound biological, psychological, social, and economic transformation — one of the most demanding developmental phases of human life. Teens navigate five major developmental challenges simultaneously: identity, autonomy, intimacy, sexuality, and achievement.

Self-injury means intentionally harming body tissue without suicidal intent. Cutting is the most common, but it includes carving, scratching, burning, biting, bruising, hitting, or picking skin and hair. It's more common in girls (over 70% in some studies), starting around ages 13–14. Approximately 15–20% of adolescents engage in self-injury at some point — higher among girls — making this far more common in teenagers than most parents realize.

Why It Happens

Self-injury isn't random. It's a way to reclaim control when everything feels chaotic. It can express bottled-up feelings, communicate unmet needs, punish perceived flaws, or cope with overwhelming sadness, anxiety, or numbness. Biologically, self-injury releases endorphins, creating a temporary "high" that can hook into addiction-like patterns.

Self-Injury vs. Suicide: A Critical Distinction

Suicide aims to end all pain. Self-injury seeks to feel better in the moment. But self-injury can lead to suicidal ideation — desperation and isolation can increase the danger over time. If you're hurting yourself, reaching out is a sign of strength, not shame.

Treatment: Building Bridges to Better Coping

Healing starts with a team: schools, parents, doctors, and mental health professionals all working together. The focus is on skill-building, reducing environmental triggers, and maintaining a completely non-judgmental atmosphere.

A comprehensive plan typically includes: individual and family therapy, CBT to rewire distorted thinking patterns, DBT (especially powerful for emotion regulation), group therapy for connection and shared understanding, and medications for underlying depression or mood instability.

What This Means for You

Breathing through the impulse (count to 10, wait 15 minutes), journaling, drawing, talking feelings out, and building positive social connections. These aren't just coping tricks — they rewire the brain over time.

If your child is self-injuring, the most important thing you can do is stay calm and stay present. Panic or anger in that moment will drive the behavior underground. Listen first. Guide to professional help second. Recovery from self-injury is genuinely possible — many young people build lasting coping skills and emerge from this period significantly stronger.

What This Means for You

- Self-injury is not attention-seeking — it is a coping mechanism for overwhelming emotion. Responding with anger or punishment pushes the behavior further underground.
- Self-injury and suicidal intent are not the same thing — but self-injury does raise the risk of suicidal thinking over time. Take it seriously.
- If you discover your child is self-injuring, stay calm. Your reaction in that moment determines whether they feel safe telling you more.
- DBT (Dialectical Behavior Therapy) has the strongest evidence base for self-injury in adolescents. Ask specifically for a DBT-trained therapist.
- Long sleeves in summer, unexplained wounds, or withdrawal from activities they used to enjoy are warning signs worth following up on.

CHAPTER THIRTEEN

SUBSTANCE USE DISORDERS

Navigating the Slippery Slope in Youth

Navigating the Slippery Slope in Youth

Substance use disorders (SUD) don't discriminate — they snag young people across every zip code, family background, and income level. SUD isn't about "weakness" or "bad choices" — it's a public health crisis fueled by biology, brain wiring, and life pressures.

Why Teens Are Especially Vulnerable

Adolescence is prime time for substance use to take root — 9 in 10 people with SUD started before age 18. The teen brain is like a sports car with a powerful accelerator but underdeveloped brakes. The reward system is primed for novelty and sensation, while the prefrontal cortex isn't fully developed until the mid-20s. Substances hit developing brains harder, with greater vulnerability to lasting damage and addiction.

Risk Factors — Including a New One Parents Often Miss

Well-established risk factors include drug-using friends (one of the strongest direct predictors), low grades or weak school connection, feeling unloved or unattached to parents, lax supervision, parental substance use, depression, anxiety, and chaotic neighborhoods.

But there is a risk factor that has moved to the front of my clinical concern in recent years: high-potency cannabis.

What This Means for You

Many parents grew up when marijuana was seen as relatively benign. That perception is now dangerously out of date. Average THC in cannabis flower has risen from roughly 3–5% in the 1990s to 15–30% or higher today — with concentrates and extracts reaching 60–90%. This is a categorically different substance. In my practice, I have seen a striking rise in teenagers presenting with new-onset psychosis and severe anxiety directly tied to heavy cannabis use. Many require inpatient psychiatric hospitalization — not because of a pre-existing disorder, but because high-potency cannabis triggered one. "It's just weed" is no longer an adequate response.

Screening: The CRAFFT Tool

A widely used screening tool for ages 12–18 is the CRAFFT. Two or more "yes" answers indicates high risk:

- C — Have you ever ridden in a Car driven by someone who was high or drunk?
- R — Do you ever use substances to Relax, fit in, or feel better?
- A — Do you ever use substances Alone?
- F — Do you ever Forget things you did while using substances?
- F — Have Family or Friends ever told you to cut down?
- T — Have you ever gotten into Trouble while using substances?

Treatment: A Team-Based Approach

Effective treatment is multimodal and team-based. Abstinence is the goal, and it is realistic with the right support structure. Group therapy tends to work particularly well. Family involvement is not optional — it's central. Relapses are part of the process, not signs of failure. And one of the most impactful steps a teen can take is replacing drug-using friendships with healthier peer connections.

Non-judgmental conversations open doors. Lecturing and shaming close them. Your relationship with your teenager is the single most powerful prevention tool available — more than any program or intervention.

What This Means for You

- Nine in ten people with a substance use disorder started using before age 18. Prevention in the early teen years is the highest-leverage window.
- "It's just weed" is no longer an adequate response. Today's high-potency cannabis can trigger psychosis and severe anxiety in the developing adolescent brain.
- Two or more "yes" answers on the CRAFFT screening tool (in this chapter) means it is time for a fuller clinical evaluation.
- Non-judgmental conversations open doors; lecturing and shaming close them. Your relationship with your teenager is your most powerful prevention tool — invest in it every day.
- Recovery from substance use disorder is possible, and relapse is a normal part of the recovery process — not a sign of failure.

CHAPTER FOURTEEN

BEYOND THERAPY

When Medication Matters

As a child psychiatrist, one of the most common concerns I hear from parents is about medication. And I want to say clearly: your concern is valid. Medication is a serious decision, and side effects are real. But I also want you to know this — if these medications did not work, they would not exist. They are used across the world because they help patients and, in many cases, they save lives. The goal of this chapter is not to push medication, but to help you understand when it is truly necessary and how to think about it clearly and without fear.

Medication Categories: A Quick Framework

Psychiatric medications for children fall into several broad categories, each addressing different types of symptoms. Understanding these categories helps parents approach the conversation with their child's prescriber with more confidence.

Medications for Depression and Anxiety

SSRIs (selective serotonin reuptake inhibitors) are the first-line treatment for both depression and anxiety in children. When SSRIs do not provide adequate relief, SNRIs (serotonin-norepinephrine reuptake inhibitors) are often tried next. For depression specifically, fluoxetine (Prozac) and escitalopram (Lexapro) have FDA approval for use in children. For anxiety disorders, sertraline (Zoloft) is frequently used in clinical practice and generally works well. Other SSRIs may be prescribed off-label — meaning they are not FDA-approved for children specifically, but clinical experience and adult data support their use in pediatric practice. It is important to note that children are more sensitive to medication side effects than adults. Careful dosing, gradual titration, and close monitoring are essential at every stage of treatment.

Medications for Psychosis

Antipsychotic medications address hallucinations, delusions, and severe disorganization. They are typically used for conditions such as early-onset schizophrenia, psychosis secondary to other medical or psychiatric conditions, and severe mood dysregulation with psychotic features.

Medications for Mood Dysregulation and Bipolar Disorder

This category includes three main types: anticonvulsants (medications originally developed for seizure disorders that also stabilize mood), antipsychotics (which carry mood-stabilizing properties in addition to their antipsychotic effects), and lithium — a unique mood stabilizer in a category of its own. Risperidone and lithium have FDA approval for pediatric use in mood disorders. It is important to understand that FDA approval does not mean a medication is the most effective option available — it means the medication has been studied and the FDA determined that its benefits outweigh its risks based on the available evidence. Many medications used off-label in this category have strong clinical data supporting their effectiveness in children.

Medications for ADHD

Stimulant medications — including methylphenidate and amphetamine-based formulations — are the primary treatment for ADHD and are among the most extensively researched medications in all of psychiatry. Non-stimulant options such as atomoxetine and alpha-agonists like guanfacine are also effective and are often preferred when stimulants are not tolerated or when co-occurring anxiety or tics are present.

A Note on Side Effects Across All Categories

Every medication in these categories carries potential side effects. Some are mild and resolve within the first few weeks; others require ongoing monitoring through regular follow-up appointments and, where indicated, blood work. Open communication between families and prescribers about any changes in mood, behavior, or physical symptoms is an essential part of safe medication management — and is discussed in more detail throughout this chapter.

Medication Is the Last Resort — But Sometimes It Is Necessary

Not every psychiatric problem in a child requires medication. Therapy, behavioral interventions, family support, and school accommodations should always be explored first. Medication enters the picture when those efforts have not been enough, when the child's safety is at risk, or when the severity of symptoms is blocking the child from developing, learning, or functioning in daily life.

The decision to try medication must be based on good rationale and genuine need. Before any medication is considered, a thorough evaluation should take place and several questions should be answered:

- Has therapy been tried adequately and for a reasonable period of time?
- How urgent is the situation — is there a safety concern?
- Is the child's learning, development, or daily functioning being significantly blocked?
- What else has been tried?
- What are the specific goals we are hoping medication will help achieve?

These are the questions that guide a responsible clinical decision.

When Medication Becomes Necessary

Severe Depression with Suicide Risk

Imagine a fifteen-year-old girl who has been in therapy for eight weeks. She is seeing a skilled therapist, but she is still having suicidal thoughts. She has made two attempts. Her therapist is working hard to build trust and connection, but that relationship takes time to develop. In the meantime, she remains at serious risk.

This is the reality of severe depression with active suicidality. Adolescents are impulsive by nature, and impulsivity combined with suicidal thoughts can be lethal. Therapy is essential and irreplaceable, but it takes time to work. Medication in this scenario is not replacing therapy — it is buying the child safety while therapy has a chance to take hold. It quiets the intensity of those thoughts enough so that she can actually engage with her therapist and begin to heal. Without that window, the risk remains dangerously high.

Neurodevelopmental Disorders and Academic Crisis

Children with ADHD or autism spectrum disorder who are struggling severely in school present another situation where medication often becomes necessary. These children are not choosing to fail. They are drowning. They may be facing suspension or expulsion. They may be so far behind academically that they are losing confidence and hope. No matter how much the teacher tries, no matter how many accommodations are put in place, if the underlying neurological barriers are not addressed, the child cannot access learning.

Some parents make the choice not to medicate, and that is their right. But it is important to be honest about what that choice requires. In homes where medication is declined without a solid alternative plan in place, what often happens is a cycle of frustration. Parents find themselves correcting the child constantly, raising their voices, repeating instructions, and managing meltdowns. Over time, this constant correction creates fear in the child and damages the parent-child relationship — the very relationship that is the foundation of everything else. The alternative to medication is not neutrality. It requires a deep commitment to patience, consistency, and structured support. For many families, medication helps restore calm so that connection and learning can actually happen.

Autism with Self-Injurious Behavior and Aggression

Children on the autism spectrum who experience significant self-injurious behaviors, intense irritability, or aggression that blocks their ability to learn and communicate face a particularly challenging situation. When a child is consumed by that level of distress, they cannot focus on developing language, building skills, or learning to self-soothe. Their window for growth is being closed by the severity of their symptoms.

In these cases, medication can reduce the intensity of those behaviors enough to open that window again. It is not about changing who the child is. It is about giving them enough relief from overwhelming internal distress that they can begin to make progress — toward communication, toward independence, toward a better quality of life.

Understanding Side Effects

When parents hear the word "medication," side effects are often the first concern. This is understandable. Let us walk through what parents actually need to know about the most commonly used medications in child psychiatry.

Medication Class	**Key Points for Parents**
SSRIs (for depression & anxiety)	Generally well tolerated. Early side effects like nausea or headaches typically ease within 1–2 weeks. The FDA black box warning flags a small increased risk of suicidal thinking early in treatment — close monitoring in the first weeks is essential.
Mood stabilizers & antipsychotics (for mood dysregulation, ASD-related irritability)	Can be highly effective. Carry a risk of weight gain and metabolic changes that require regular monitoring. Side effects can be managed with regular monitoring and follow-up.
Stimulants (for ADHD)	Among the most well-researched treatments in all of psychiatry. Untreated ADHD actually increases addiction risk over time — appropriately used stimulants can reduce that risk by helping children succeed and build self-regulation skills.

What This Means for You

The antidepressant black box warning does not mean medication causes suicide. It means that close monitoring in the early weeks is essential. Any changes in mood or behavior should be reported to the prescribing provider immediately. This monitoring, done well, is part of what makes treatment safe.

Individualized Decision-Making

In all cases, the choice of medication is always individualized. Every child is different, every clinical situation is unique, and the risk-benefit ratio must always be carefully weighed by the clinician, the parents, and when appropriate, the child.

The goal is never to medicate for convenience. The goal is always to give the child the best possible chance at a healthy, connected, and fulfilling life.

What This Means for You

- Medication is not the first resort — but when therapy alone isn't enough, or when safety is at risk, it can be genuinely life-saving.
- SSRIs for anxiety and depression are generally well tolerated. Early side effects like nausea usually resolve within 1–2 weeks.
- The FDA black box warning on antidepressants does not mean medication causes suicide — it means close monitoring in the early weeks is essential.
- Stimulants for ADHD are among the most studied treatments in all of psychiatry. Used correctly, they reduce — not increase — the long-term risk of addiction.
- Medication works best alongside therapy, not instead of it. The two together produce the strongest and most lasting outcomes.
- Your questions and concerns about medication are valid. A good prescriber will welcome them and work through them with you.

CHAPTER FIFTEEN

NAVIGATING THE DIGITAL WORLD

Smart Guidelines for Social Media and Your Family's Mental Health

Social media can be a genuine connector — sharing laughs, staying in touch, building support networks. But for kids and teens whose brains are still developing impulse control and self-image, it can be a minefield. Cyberbullying, comparison traps, and endless dopamine hits from likes can fuel anxiety, depression, and body image issues.

Practical Guidelines That Actually Work

1. Make Parents or Guardians Your "Friends" Online: Accept a parent or guardian as a friend or follower on all platforms. This builds trust and accountability — not to snoop, but to guide and protect.

2. Share Passwords Only With Trusted Adults: Passwords should be shared with parents or caregivers — but kept strictly confidential otherwise. If a "friend" gets your login, they could post harmful content under your name.

3. Post With the "Grandma Test" in Mind: Before posting anything, ask: Would I want my grandma, teacher, or future employer to see this? Assume it could go viral — because it might.

4. Keep Photos Positive and Private: Skip posting pictures that could reflect badly on you, your friends, or your family. Even "friends-only" settings aren't foolproof — one share and it's permanent.

5. Don't "Like" or Repost Negativity: Clicking "like" on a mean or defamatory post is co-signing it — with the same fallout as if you wrote it. Curate your feed toward uplifting content.

6. No Secret Accounts or Hidden Changes: Transparency prevents hidden online lives that could conceal bullying, grooming, or escalating mental health struggles.

7. These Rules Apply Across All Platforms: Consistency matters. Whether it's Instagram, TikTok, Snapchat, or text messages, the same values apply everywhere.

Implementing These Guidelines

Start with a family meeting — make it collaborative so kids feel heard, not dictated to. Tie rules to privileges: follow them and access stays; break them and there are fair, consistent consequences. Track mental health signs: if social media is consistently amplifying irritability, withdrawal, or body obsession, it may be time for professional input.

These guidelines are about empowerment, not restriction. They protect growing minds and build resilience for the real world.

What This Means for You

- Social media is not inherently harmful — but without structure and conversation, it can amplify anxiety, depression, and body image struggles in vulnerable teens.
- The "Grandma Test" is genuinely useful: before posting anything, ask whether you'd be comfortable with the whole world seeing it.
- Following your child on social media is not spying — it is parenting in the digital age. Frame it as trust-building, not surveillance.
- If social media is consistently triggering irritability, withdrawal, or obsessive behavior in your child, reduce access and seek professional input.
- Have the conversation about online safety early and often — not as a one-time lecture, but as an ongoing, open dialogue.

CHAPTER SIXTEEN

TIPS FOR PARENTS

Behavioral Strategies to Support Your Child at Home and School

These aren't "magic fixes," but evidence-based tools that empower you to create calmer, more connected days. Recent research shows these approaches can reduce disruptive behaviors by 30–50% and significantly boost parenting confidence.

Why These Strategies Work

Children's behaviors — from tantrums to task avoidance — often stem from unmet needs, overwhelm, or genuine skill gaps, especially in neurodiverse children. The framework breaks into three categories: Prevention (nip triggers before they erupt), Replacement (teach better skills), and Response (reinforce good behavior, handle difficult behavior consistently).

Prevention Strategies: Altering the Environment

<u>Visual supports and routines:</u> Create visual schedules with picture cards outlining daily activities. Give 5–10 minute warnings before transitions using timers. Share these aids with teachers so the same structure exists at school. Predictability is calming — it dramatically reduces anxiety and frustration in children with ASD and ADHD.

<u>Breaking tasks into manageable steps</u>: Split homework into 5–10 minute chunks with built-in breaks. Weave in your child's interests wherever possible. Ask teachers to provide checklists and pre-chunked assignments. This minimizes overwhelm and reduces the number of redirections needed.

Replacement Strategies: Teaching Better Skills

<u>Emotion regulation and coping techniques:</u> Teach deep breathing and simple "calm-down" phrases — "I need a break" or "This is hard for me" — through role-play during calm moments, not crisis moments. Practice makes these tools automatic when stress hits.

<u>Functional communication and problem-solving:</u> Use picture boards or scripts to help children request help instead of melting down. Research on functional communication training shows 25–35% reductions in disruptive behaviors.

Response Strategies: Reinforcing Positive Behaviors

Positive reinforcement and consistent consequences: Offer immediate praise or small rewards — a sticker chart leading to screen time — for task completion or use of coping skills. Safely ignore minor attention-seeking behaviors (responding to them reinforces them). Token economies work well at school.

Time-outs or loss of privileges for escalations: For severe irritability, use brief, calm time-outs (1 minute per year of age) without extra attention, then redirect to a positive activity. The key is calm and consistent — emotional escalation on the parent's part models the opposite of what you're teaching.

Putting It Into Action: Your Parental Playbook

Start small — pick one strategy from each category and track progress over 2 weeks before adding more. For home: build daily routines with visual supports. At school: share your strategies with teachers and ensure consistency — collaboration between home and school boosts outcomes by 20–30%.

The Bottom Line

Not every day will be a win — relapses happen, and consistency over time is what matters. Even parent-only training (without direct child involvement) consistently improves child functioning by about 50% while reducing parental stress. These strategies empower you as a parent — prevention calms the storms before they start, replacement strategies build lasting skills, and response strategies reinforce growth day by day.

If behaviors consistently overwhelm despite these tools, a therapist or pediatric psychiatrist can provide a tailored plan. Keep nurturing that connection — it matters more than any technique.

What This Means for You

- Prevention is easier than intervention — setting up predictable routines and visual supports before behavior escalates saves enormous stress.
- Start with one strategy, not ten. Pick one tool from prevention, one from replacement, and one from response. Track it for two weeks before adding more.
- Collaboration between home and school is one of the highest-leverage moves available. When parents and teachers use the same system, outcomes improve by 20–30%.
- Consistency matters more than perfection. A good-enough response, applied reliably every day, beats an ideal response applied sporadically.
- If you feel overwhelmed, that is not a sign of failure — it is a signal to get support. Parent training programs exist precisely because this is hard, and they work.

A FINAL WORD

Mental health is not a destination — it's a journey, and no one travels it alone. Whether you're a parent watching closely, a young person navigating hard days, or an adult making sense of your past, the fact that you're reading this matters.

Understanding is the beginning of everything. It's what turns fear into compassion, confusion into clarity, and isolation into connection. Each chapter in this book has been written with one goal: to give you the knowledge to recognize what's happening and the confidence to reach out for help.

Early support changes outcomes. Compassionate understanding changes lives. You — and the people you love — are absolutely worth fighting for.

— Dr. Faisal Ahmed, MD

Board-Certified Child and Adolescent Psychiatrist

California

DISCLAIMER

The information contained in this book is intended for general educational and informational purposes only. It is not a substitute for professional medical advice, diagnosis, or treatment. Always seek the guidance of a qualified healthcare provider — including a licensed physician, psychiatrist, psychologist, or other mental health professional — with any questions you may have regarding a medical or psychiatric condition.

Nothing in this book should be interpreted as establishing a physician-patient relationship between the author and the reader. The clinical examples and case illustrations described in this book have been de-identified and modified to protect patient confidentiality. Any resemblance to specific individuals is coincidental.

The author has made every effort to ensure that the information presented is accurate and consistent with current standards at the time of publication. However, medical knowledge evolves, and readers are encouraged to consult up-to-date clinical resources and qualified professionals for guidance specific to their circumstances.

This book is not intended to be used as a basis for legal, financial, or regulatory decisions. The author and publisher expressly disclaim any liability arising directly or indirectly from the use or application of any information contained in this book.

ABOUT THE AUTHOR

Faisal Ahmed, MD

Staff Psychiatrist | Vice Chief of Staff, Sutter Center for Psychiatry

Dr. Faisal Ahmed is a board-certified psychiatrist with subspecialty certification in child and adolescent psychiatry through the American Board of Psychiatry and Neurology. He completed his residency training in general psychiatry and his fellowship in child and adolescent psychiatry at the University of Missouri, Columbia.

Dr. Ahmed brings extensive clinical experience across a broad range of psychiatric settings, including outpatient, inpatient, and consultation-liaison services. His clinical interests include psychological trauma, neurodevelopmental disorders — including ADHD and autism spectrum disorder — and psychopharmacology.

A dedicated educator, Dr. Ahmed has contributed to graduate medical education at multiple institutions, including Lutheran General Hospital's Psychiatry Residency Training Program, Advocate BroMenn Medical Center's Family Medicine Residency Program, and ATSU-KCOM, The Kirksville College of Osteopathic Medicine, where he served as an official clinical preceptor. He currently holds a Volunteer Clinical Faculty appointment at UC Davis School of Medicine.

Dr. Ahmed currently serves as a staff psychiatrist and Vice Chief of Staff at Sutter Center for Psychiatry, where he is committed to training the next generation of compassionate, clinically excellent psychiatrists.

ABOUT THE BOOK

Every parent has felt it — that moment of uncertainty when you watch your child and wonder: Is this normal? Should I be worried? Am I doing enough? The questions are universal. The clear, trustworthy answers have been harder to find. Until now.

In The Heart of the Matter, board-certified child and adolescent psychiatrist Dr. Faisal Ahmed offers parents and caregivers an honest, compassionate, and clinically grounded guide to understanding children's mental health. Drawing on decades of clinical experience, Dr. Ahmed walks readers through the full arc of child development — from infancy through adolescence — and then addresses the conditions that most commonly disrupt it: ADHD, anxiety, trauma, autism spectrum disorder, depression, bipolar disorder, eating disorders, self-injury, substance use, and more.

Written in the same direct, warm voice Dr. Ahmed uses with families in his office, this book replaces fear and confusion with clarity and practical tools. Each chapter closes with a "What This Means For You" section — concrete, actionable guidance that parents can use immediately. Whether you are navigating a new diagnosis, trying to understand a child who seems different, or simply want to be more informed and present, this book was written for you.

Understanding is the beginning of everything. It's what turns fear into compassion, confusion into clarity, and isolation into connection.

www.ingramcontent.com/pod-product-compliance
Lightning Source LLC
LaVergne TN
LVHW050923210926
848482LV00012B/510

* 9 7 9 8 9 9 9 2 0 5 3 4 6 *